**The critics applaud Ntozake Shange's
*for colored girls who have considered suicide/
when the rainbow is enuf***

"Overwhelming. . . . It's joyous and alive, affirmative in the face of despair."
—Douglas Watt, *New York Daily News*

"Passionate and lyrical. . . . In poetry and prose Shange describes what it means to be a black woman in a world of mean streets, deceitful men and aching loss."
—Allan Wallach, *Newsday*

"These poems and prose selections are . . . rich with the author's special voice: **by turns bitter, funny, ironic, and savage; fiercely honest and personal.**"
—Martin Gottfried, *New York Post*

"Ntozake Shange's extraordinary 'choreopoem' . . . is **a dramatic elegy for black women with an undercurrent message for everyone.** Its theme is not sorrow . . . but courage. Its strength is its passion and its reality. . . . **An unforgettable collage of one woman's view of the women of her race,** facing everything from rape to unrequited love. . . . Wisdom and naivete go hand in hand. Wounds and dreams intermingle; strong passions melt into simple courage."
—William A. Raidy, *L.I. Press/Newhouse Newspapers*

"Remember when poetry used to give you chills, make you tremble? Ntozake Shange writes that kind of rousing poetry. It **has the power to move a body to tears, to rage, and to an ultimate rush of love.**"
—Marilyn Stasio, *Cue magazine*

"Ntozake Shange's poetry approaches the force of a whirlwind."
—*Encore American & Worldwide News*

also by ntozake shange

theater

three pieces
spell #7
a photograph: lovers in motion
boogie woogie landscapes

poetry

nappy edges
a daughter's geography
ridin' the moon in texas
the love space demands

fiction

sassafrass, cypress & indigo
betsey brown
liliane

for colored girls who have considered suicide/ when the rainbow is enuf

a choreopoem/

ntozake shange

scribner poetry

for the spirits of my grandma
viola benzena murray owens
and my great aunt
effie owens josey

SCRIBNER POETRY
SCRIBNER
1230 Avenue of the Americas
New York, NY 10020

This book is a work of fiction. Names, characters, places, and incidents either are products of the author's imagination or are used fictitiously. Any resemblance to actual events or locales or persons, living or dead, is entirely coincidental.

Copyright © 1975, 1976, 1977 by Ntozake Shange

All rights reserved, including the right of reproduction in whole or in part in any form.

First Scribner Poetry edition 1997

SCRIBNER POETRY and design are trademarks of Macmillan Library Reference USA, Inc., used under license by Simon & Schuster, the publisher of this work.

Manufactured in the United States of America

20 19 18 17 16 15

The Library of Congress has cataloged the Collier edition as follows:
Shange, Ntozake.
For colored girls who have considered suicide when the rainbow is enuf : a choreopoem / Ntozake Shange. —1st Collier Books ed.
p.   cm.
I. Title.
[PS3569.H3324F6   1989]
811'.54—dc19   88-32633
CIP

ISBN-13: 978-0-684-84326-1
ISBN-10:   0-684-84326-9

Amateur and professional performance rights to this play are controlled by Samuel French, Inc., 45 West 25th Street, New York, NY 10010, and must be procured before proceeding with production. *Please Note:* Special publicity posters are available. Write to Samuel French, Inc., for details.

poems by title

dark phrases 3

graduation nite 7

now i love somebody more than 11

no assistance 13

i'm a poet who 14

latent rapists' 17

abortion cycle #1 22

sechita 23

toussaint 25

one 31

i used to live in the world 36

pyramid 39

no more love poems #1 42

no more love poems #2 43

no more love poems #3 44

no more love poems #4 45

somebody almost walked off wid alla my stuff 49

sorry 52

a nite with beau willie brown 55

a laying on of hands 60

for colored girls who have considered suicide/ when the rainbow is enuf was first presented at the Bacchanal, a woman's bar just outside Berkeley, California. With Paula Moss & Elvia Marta who worked with me in Raymond Sawyer's Afro-American Dance Company & Halifu's The Spirit of Dance; Nashira Ntosha, a guitarist & program coordinator at KPOO-FM (one of the few Bay Area stations focusing on women's programming); Jessica Hagedorn, a poet & reading tour companion; & Joanna Griffin, co-founder of the Bacchanal, publisher of Effie's Press, & a poet. We just did it. Working in bars waz a circumstantial aesthetic of poetry in San Francisco from Spec's, an old beat hangout, to 'new' Malvina's, Minnie's Can-Do Club, the Coffee Gallery, & the Rippletad. With as much space as a small studio on the Lower East Side, the five of us, five women, proceeded to dance, make poems, make music, make a woman's theater for about twenty patrons. This was December of 1974. We were a little raw, self-conscious, & eager. Whatever we were discovering in ourselves that nite had been in process among us for almost two years.

I first met Jessica & Nashira thru Third World Communications (The Woman's Collective) when the first anthology of Third World women writers in the U.S.A. was published. With Janice Mirikitani, Avotcja, Carol Lee Sanchez, Janet Campbell Hale, Kitty Tsui, Janic Cobb, Thulani, and a score more, San Francisco waz inundated with women poets, women's readings, & a multilingual woman presence, new to all of us & desperately appreciated. The force of these readings on all our lives waz to become evident as we directed our energies toward clarifying our lives—& the lives of our mothers, daughters, & grandmothers— as women. During the same period, Shameless Hussy Press & The Oakland Women's Press Collective were also reading anywhere & everywhere they could. In a single season, Susan Griffin, Judy Grahn, Barbara Gravelle, & Alta, were promoting the poetry & presence of women in a legendary male-poet's environment. This is the energy & part of the style that nurtured *for colored girls* . . .

More stable as a source of inspiration & historical continuity waz the Women's Studies Program at Sonoma State College, where I worked with J. J. Wilson, Joanna Griffin, & Wopo Holup over a three year span. Courses designed to make women's lives & dynamics familiar to us, such as: Woman as Artist; Woman as Poet; Androgynous Myths in Literature; Women's Biography I & II; Third World Women Writers, are inextricably bound to the development of my sense of the world, myself, & women's language. Studying the mythology of women from antiquity to the present day led directly to the piece *Sechita* in which a dance hall girl is perceived as deity, as slut, as innocent & knowing. Unearthing the mislaid, forgotten, &/or misunderstood women writers, painters, mothers, cowgirls, & union leaders of our pasts proved to be both a supportive experience & a challenge not to let them down, not to do less than—at all costs not be less woman than—our mothers, from Isis to Marie Laurencin, Zora Neale Hurtson to Kathe Kollwitz, Anna May Wong to Calamity Jane.

Such joy & excitement I knew in Sonoma, then I would commute back the sixty miles to San Francisco to study dance with Raymond Sawyer, Ed Mock, & Halifu. Knowing a woman's mind & spirit had been allowed me, with dance I discovered my body more intimately than I had imagined possible. With the acceptance of the ethnicity of my thighs & backside, came a clearer understanding of my voice as a woman & as a poet. The freedom to move in space, to demand of my own sweat a perfection that could continually be approached, though never known, waz poem to me, my body & mind ellipsing, probably for the first time in my life. Just as Women's Studies had rooted me to an articulated female heritage & imperative, so dance as explicated by Raymond Sawyer & Ed Mock insisted that everything African, everything halfway colloquial, a grimace, a strut, an arched back over a yawn, waz mine. I moved what waz my unconscious knowledge of being in a colored woman's body to my known everydayness. The depth of my past waz made tangible to me in Sawyer's *Ananse*, a dance exploring the Diaspora to contemporary Senegalese music, pulling ancient trampled spirits out of present tense Afro-American Dance. Watching Ed Mock re-create the Step Brothers' or Bert Williams' routines in class or on stage, in black face mimicking Eddie Cantor or Gloria Swanson, being the rush of irony & control that are the foundation of jazz dance, was as startling as humbling. With Raymond Sawyer & Ed Mock, Paula Moss & I learned the wealth of our bodies, if we worked, if we opened up, if we made the dance our own.

The first experience of women's theater for me as a performer

waz the months I spent with Halifu Osumare's The Spirit of
Dance, a troupe of five to six black women who depicted the
history of Black dance from its origins in Western Africa thru to
the popular dances seen on our streets. Without a premeditated or
conscious desire to create a female piece, that's what, in fact,
Halifu did. Working in San Francisco & Berkeley public schools
as an adjunct to Ethnic Studies, I learned the mechanics of self-
production & absorbed some of Halifu's confidence in her work,
the legitimacy of our visions. After some 73 performances
with The Spirit of Dance, I left the company to begin production
of *for colored girls* . . .

In the summer of 1974 I had begun a series of seven poems,
modeled on Judy Grahn's *The Common Woman*, which were to
explore the realities of seven different kinds of women. They
were numbered pieces: the women were to be nameless & assume
hegemony as dictated by the fullness of their lives. The first of
the series is the poem, 'one' (orange butterflies & aqua sequins),
which prompted the title *& this is for colored girls who have
considered suicide/ when the rainbow is enuf*. I waz smitten by
my own language, & called all the performances I waz to give
from then on by that title. In other words, all the readings &
choreopoetry that Paula Moss & I developed after that summer waz
for colored girls. . . . We started at the Bacchanal & worked
through the winter at Ed Mock's Dance Studio with the assistance
of West Coast Dance Works, setting pieces & cleaning up
poems. I found two bands, The Sound Clinic (a horn trio) &
Jean Desarmes & His Raggae Blues Band, who agreed to work with

us if I found space. & I did. The space we used waz the space
I knew: Women's Studies Departments, bars, cafes, & poetry
centers. With the selection of poems changing, dependent upon our
audience & our mood, & the dance growing to take space of its
own, so that Paula inspired my words to fall from me with her
body, & The Sound Clinic working with new arrangements of
Ornette Coleman compositions & their own, The Raggae Blues
Band giving Caribbean renditions of Jimi Hendrix & Redding, we
set dates for Minnie's Can-Do Club in Haight-Ashbury. The
poets showed up for us, the dancers showed up for us, the
women's community showed up, & we were listed as a 'must see'
in *The Bay Guardian.* Eight days after our last weekend
at Minnie's, Paula & I left to drive cross country to New York
to do 'the show,' as we called it, at the Studio Rivbea
in New York.

Our work in San Francisco waz over. With the courage of
children, we staged the same sort of informal & improvised cho-
reopoems at Rivbea during the Summer Music Festival. Instead
of the Standing-Room-Only crowds we were accustomed to in San
Francisco, my family & a few friends came to see our great
project. One of these friends, Oz Scott, & my sister, Ifa Iyaun,
who were instrumental in the development of *for colored girls* . . .
saw the show that night. Oz offered to help me with the staging
of the work for a New York audience, since Paula & I obviously
didn't understand some things. We moved from the Rivbea
to the Old Reliable on East 3rd Street to work through some of the
ideas Oz had & the new things Paula & I were developing.

Gylan Kain of the Original Last Poets waz working there every Monday night. We worked with him & any other poets & dancers who showed up. Several members of the original New York show came to us just this haphazardly. Aku Kadogo & I both had scholarships at Diane McIntyre's Sounds-in-Motion Dance Studio. I asked her if she felt like improvising on the Lower East Side, she agreed & has been with the show ever since. Laurie Carlos stopped by one evening. She stayed. Somehow word got out & people started coming to the back room of this neighborhood bar. We were moved to a new bar down the street, DeMonte's, after eleven weeks of no-pay hard-work three sets a night—maybe a shot of cognac on the house.

The show at DeMonte's waz prophetic. By this time, December of 1975, we had weaned the piece of extraneous theatricality, enlisted Trazana Beverley, Laurie Carlos, Laurie Hayes, Aku Kadogo, & of course, Paula & I were right there. The most prescient change in the concept of the work waz that I gave up directorial powers to Oz Scott. By doing this, I acknowledged that the poems & the dance worked on their own to do & be what they were. As opposed to viewing the pieces as poems, I came to understand these twenty-odd poems as a single statement, a choreopoem.

We finally hit at DeMonte's. Those institutions I had shunned as a poet—producers, theaters, actresses, & sets—now were essential to us. *for colored girls who have considered suicide/ when the rainbow is enuf* waz a theater piece. Woody King picked up our option to produce us as a Workshop under Equity's Showcase Code at Henry Street. With the assistance of the New York Shakespeare Festival & Joe Papp, we received space & a set, lights & a mailing list, things Paula & I had done without for two years. We opened at Henry Street with two new actress-dancers, Thea Martinez & Judy Dearing. Lines of folks & talk all over the Black & Latin community propelled us to the Public Theater in June. Then to the Booth Theater on Broadway in September of 1976.

Every move we've made since the first showing of *for colored girls* . . . in California has demanded changes of text, personnel, & staging. The final production at the Booth is as close to distilled as any of us in all our art forms can make it. With two new actresses, Janet League & Rise Collins, & with the help of Seret Scott, Michelle Shay, & Roxanne Reese, the rest of the cast is enveloping almost 6,000 people a week in the words of a young black girl's growing up, her triumphs & errors, our struggle to become all that is forbidden by our environment, all that is forfeited by our gender, all that we have forgotten.

I had never imagined not doing *for colored girls*. . . . It waz just my poems, any poems I happened to have. Now I have left the show on Broadway, to write poems, stories, plays, my dreams. *for colored girls* . . . is either too big for my off-off Broadway taste, or too little for my exaggerated sense of freedom, held over from seven years of improvised poetry readings. Or, perhaps, the series has actually finished itself. Poems come on their own time: i am offering these to you as what i've received from this world so far.

i am on the other side of the rainbow/ picking up the pieces of days spent waitin for the poem to be heard/ while you listen/ i have other work to do/

ntozake shange
new york, 1976

*for colored girls who
have considered suicide/
when the rainbow is enuf*

The stage is in darkness. Harsh music is heard as dim blue lights come up. One after another, seven women run onto the stage from each of the exits. They all freeze in postures of distress. The follow spot picks up the lady in brown. She comes to life and looks around at the other ladies. All of the others are still. She walks over to the lady in red and calls to her. The lady in red makes no response.

    lady in brown
dark phrases of womanhood
of never havin been a girl
half-notes scattered
without rhythm/ no tune
distraught laughter fallin
over a black girl's shoulder
it's funny/ it's hysterical
the melody-less-ness of her dance
don't tell nobody don't tell a soul
she's dancin on beer cans & shingles

this must be the spook house
another song with no singers
lyrics/ no voices

& interrupted solos
unseen performances

are we ghouls?
children of horror?
the joke?

don't tell nobody don't tell a soul
are we animals? have we gone crazy?

i can't hear anythin
but maddening screams
& the soft strains of death
& you promised me
you promised me . . .
somebody/ anybody
sing a black girl's song
bring her out
to know herself
to know you
but sing her rhythms
carin/ struggle/ hard times
sing her song of life
she's been dead so long
closed in silence so long
she doesn't know the sound
of her own voice
her infinite beauty

she's half-notes scattered
without rhythm/ no tune
sing her sighs
sing the song of her possibilities
sing a righteous gospel
let her be born
let her be born
& handled warmly.

   lady in brown
i'm outside chicago

   lady in yellow
i'm outside detroit

   lady in purple
i'm outside houston

   lady in red
i'm outside baltimore

   lady in green
i'm outside san francisco

   lady in blue
i'm outside manhattan

   lady in orange
i'm outside st. louis

    lady in brown
& this is for colored girls who have considered suicide
but moved to the ends of their own rainbows.

    everyone
mama's little baby likes shortnin, shortnin,
mama's little baby likes shortnin bread
mama's little baby likes shortnin, shortnin,
mama's little baby likes shortnin bread

little sally walker, sittin in a saucer
rise, sally, rise, wipe your weepin eyes
an put your hands on your hips
an let your backbone slip
o, shake it to the east
o, shake it to the west
shake it to the one
that you like the best

    lady in purple
you're it

> As the lady in brown tags each of
> the other ladies they freeze. When
> each one has been tagged the lady
> in brown freezes. Immediately
> "Dancing in the Streets" by Martha
> and the Vandellas is heard. All

                    of the ladies start to dance. The
                    lady in green, the lady in blue, and
                    the lady in yellow do the pony,
                    the big boss line, the swim, and
                    the nose dive. The other ladies
                    dance in place.

   lady in yellow
it was graduation nite & i waz the only virgin in the crowd
bobby mills martin jerome & sammy yates eddie jones & randi
all cousins
all the prettiest niggers in this factory town
carried me out wit em
in a deep black buick
smellin of thunderbird & ladies in heat
we rambled from camden to mount holly
laughin at the afternoon's speeches
& danglin our tassles from the rear view mirror
climbin different sorta project stairs
movin toward snappin beer cans &
GET IT GET IT THAT'S THE WAY TO DO IT MAMA
all mercer county graduated the same nite
      cosmetology secretarial pre-college autoshop & business
all us movin from mama to what ever waz out there

that nite we raced a big ol truck from the barbeque stand
trying to tell him bout the party at jacqui's
where folks graduated last year waz waitin to hit it wid us

i got drunk & cdnt figure out
whose hand waz on my thigh/ but it didn't matter
cuz these cousins martin eddie sammy jerome & bobby
waz my sweethearts alternately since the seventh grade
& everybody knew i always started cryin if somebody actually
tried to take advantage of me
    at jacqui's
ulinda mason was stickin her mouth all out
while we tumbled out the buick
eddie jones waz her lickin stick
but i knew how to dance
    it got soo hot
vincent ramos puked all in the punch
& harly jumped all in tico's face
cuz he was leavin for the navy in the mornin
hadda kick ass so we'd all remember how bad he waz
seems like sheila & marguerite waz fraid
to get their hair turnin back
so they laid up against the wall
lookin almost sexy
didnt wanna sweat
but me & my fellas   we waz dancin

since 1963 i'd won all kinda contests
wid the cousins at the POLICE ATHLETIC LEAGUE DANCES
all mercer county knew
any kin to martin yates cd turn somersaults
fore smokey robinson cd get a woman excited

The Dells singing "Stay" is heard

we danced   doin nasty ol tricks

> *The lady in yellow sings along with the Dells for a moment. The lady in orange and the lady in blue jump up and parody the lady in yellow and the Dells. The lady in yellow stares at them. They sit down.*

doin nasty ol tricks i'd been thinkin since may
cuz graduation nite had to be hot
& i waz the only virgin
so i hadda make like my hips waz inta some business
that way everybody thot whoever was gettin it
was a older man cdnt run the streets wit youngsters
martin slipped his leg round my thigh
the dells bumped "stay"
up & down—up & down the new carver homes
WE WAZ GROWN   WE WAZ FINALLY GROWN

ulinda alla sudden went crazy
went over to eddie cursin & carryin on
tearin his skin wid her nails
the cousins tried to talk sense to her
tried to hold her arms
lissin bitch sammy went on

bobby whispered i shd go wit him
fore they go ta cuttin
fore the police arrived
we teetered silently thru the parkin lot
no un uhuh
we didn't know nothin bout no party
bobby started lookin at me
yeah
he started looking at me real strange
like i waz a woman or somethin/
started talkin real soft
in the backseat of that ol buick
WOW
by daybreak
i just cdnt stop grinnin.

The Dells singing "Stay" comes in and all of the ladies except the lady in blue join in and sing along.

    lady in blue
you gave it up in a buick?

    lady in yellow
yeh, and honey, it was wonderful.

    lady in green
we used to do it all up in the dark
in the corners . . .

10/

lady in blue
some niggah sweating all over you.

lady in red
it was good!

lady in blue
i never did like to grind.

lady in yellow
what other kind of dances are there?

lady in blue
mambo, bomba, merengue

when i waz sixteen i ran off to the south bronx
cuz i waz gonna meet up wit willie colon
& dance all the time
                      mamba bomba merengue
lady in yellow
do you speak spanish?

lady in blue
olà
my papa thot he was puerto rican & we wda been
cept we waz just reglar niggahs wit hints of spanish
so off i made it to this 36 hour marathon dance
con salsa con ricardo
'suggggggggggar' ray on southern blvd

next door to this fotografi place
jammed wit burial weddin & communion relics
next door to la real ideal genuine spanish barber
            up up up up up stairs & stairs & lotsa hallway
wit my colored new jersey self
didn't know what anybody waz saying
cept if dancin waz proof of origin
         i was jibarita herself that nite
& the next day
i kept smilin & right on steppin
if he cd lead i waz ready to dance
if he cdnt lead
i caught this attitude
         i'd seen rosa do
& wd not be bothered
i waz twirlin hippin givin much quik feet
& bein a mute cute colored puerto rican
til saturday afternoon when the disc-jockey say
'SORRY FOLKS WILLIE COLON AINT GONNA MAKE IT TODAY'
& alla my niggah temper came outta control
& i wdnt dance wit nobody
& i talked english loud
& i love you more than i waz mad
uh huh uh huh
more than more than
when i discovered archie shepp & subtle blues
doncha know i wore out the magic of juju
heroically resistin being possessed

ooooooooooooooh the sounds
sneakin in under age to slug's
to stare ata real 'artiste'
& every word outta imamu's mouth waz gospel
& if jesus cdnt play a horn like shepp
waznt no need for colored folks to bear no cross at all

& poem is my thank-you for music
& i love you more than poem
more than aureliano buendia loved macondo
more than hector lavoe loved himself
more than the lady loved gardenias
more than celia loves cuba or graciela loves el son
more than the flamingoes shoo-do-n-doo-wah love bein pretty

oyè négro
te amo mas que   te amo mas que
when you play
yr flute

    everyone (very softly)
te amo mas que   te amo mas que

    lady in red
without any assistance or guidance from you
i have loved you assiduously for 8 months 2 wks & a day
i have been stood up four times
i've left 7 packages on yr doorstep

forty poems 2 plants & 3 handmade notecards i left
town so i cd send to you have been no help to me
on my job
you call at 3:00 in the mornin on weekdays
so i cd drive 27½ miles cross the bay before i go to work
charmin charmin
but you are of no assistance
i want you to know
this waz an experiment
to see how selfish i cd be
if i wd really carry on to snare a possible lover
if i waz capable of debasin my self for the love of another
if i cd stand not being wanted
when i wanted to be wanted
& i cannot
so
with no further assistance & no guidance from you
i am endin this affair

this note is attached to a plant
i've been waterin since the day i met you
you may water it
yr damn self

   lady in orange
i dont wanna write
in english or spanish
i wanna sing   make you dance
like the bata   dance   scream

twitch hips wit me cuz
i done forgot all abt words
aint got no definitions
i wanna whirl
           with you

                      Music starts, "Che Che Cole" by
                      Willie Colon.
                      Everyone starts to dance.

our whole body
wrapped like a ripe mango
ramblin whippin thru space
on the corner in the park
where the rug useta be
let willie colon take you out
swing your head
push your leg to the moon with me

i'm on the lower east side
in new york city
and i can't   i can't
talk witchu no more

    lady in yellow
we gotta dance to keep from cryin

    lady in brown
we gotta dance to keep from dyin

  lady in red
so come on

  lady in brown
come on

  lady in purple
come on

  lady in orange
hold yr head like it was ruby sapphire
i'm a poet
who writes in english
come to share the worlds witchu

  everyone
come to share our worlds witchu
we come here to be dancin
    to be dancin
   to be dancin
  baya

        There is a sudden light change, all
        of the ladies react as if they had
        been struck in the face. The lady in
        green and the lady in yellow run
        out up left, the lady in orange runs
        out the left volm, the lady in
        brown runs out up right.

    lady in blue
a friend is hard to press charges against

    lady in red
if you know him
you must have wanted it

    lady in purple
a misunderstanding

    lady in red
you know
these things happen

    lady in blue
are you sure
you didnt suggest

    lady in purple
had you been drinkin

    lady in red
a rapist is always to be a stranger
to be legitimate
someone you never saw
a man wit obvious problems

    lady in purple
pin-ups attached to the insides of his lapels

 lady in blue
ticket stubs from porno flicks in his pocket

 lady in purple
a lil dick

 lady in red
or a strong mother

 lady in blue
or just a brutal virgin

 lady in red
but if you've been seen in public wit him
danced one dance
kissed him good-bye lightly

 lady in purple
wit closed mouth

 lady in blue
pressin charges will be as hard
as keepin yr legs closed
while five fools try to run a train on you

 lady in red
these men friends of ours
who smile nice

stay employed
and take us out to dinner

    lady in purple
lock the door behind you

    lady in blue
wit fist in face
to fuck

    lady in red
who make elaborate mediterranean dinners
& let the art ensemble carry all ethical burdens
while they invite a coupla friends over to have you
are sufferin from latent rapist bravado
& we are left wit the scars

    lady in blue
bein betrayed by men who know us

    lady in purple
& expect
like the stranger
we always thot waz comin

    lady in blue
that we will submit

    lady in purple
we must have known

    lady in red
women relinquish all personal rights
in the presence of a man
who apparently cd be considered a rapist

    lady in purple
especially if he has been considered a friend

    lady in blue
& is no less worthy of bein beat witin an inch of his life
bein publicly ridiculed
havin two fists shoved up his ass

    lady in red
than the stranger
we always thot it wd be

    lady in blue
who never showed up

    lady in red
cuz it turns out the nature of rape has changed

    lady in blue
we can now meet them in circles we frequent for companionship

   lady in purple
we see them at the coffeehouse

   lady in blue
wit someone else we know

   lady in red
we cd even have em over for dinner
& get raped in our own houses
by invitation
a friend

> *The lights change, and the ladies are all hit by an imaginary slap, the lady in red runs off up left.*

   lady in blue
eyes

   lady in purple
mice

   lady in blue
womb

   lady in blue & lady in purple
nobody

> *The lady in purple exits up right.*

lady in blue
tubes tables white washed windows
grime from age wiped over once
legs spread
anxious
eyes crawlin up on me
eyes rollin in my thighs
metal horses gnawin my womb
dead mice fall from my mouth
i really didnt mean to
i really didnt think i cd
just one day off . . .
get offa me alla this blood
bones shattered like soft ice-cream cones

i cdnt have people
lookin at me
pregnant
i cdnt have my friends see this
dyin danglin tween my legs
& i didnt say a thing
not a sigh
or a fast scream
to get
those eyes offa me
get them steel rods outta me
this hurts
this hurts me

& nobody came
cuz nobody knew
once i waz pregnant & shamed of myself.

> The lady in blue exits stage left
> volm.
>
> Soft deep music is heard, voices
> calling "Sechita" come from the
> wings and volms. The lady in
> purple enters from up right.

    lady in purple
once there were quadroon balls/ elegance in st. louis/ laced
mulattoes/ gamblin down the mississippi/ to memphis/ new
orleans n okra crepes near the bayou/ where the poor white trash
wd sing/ moanin/ strange/ liquid tones/ thru the swamps/

> The lady in green enters from the
> right volm; she is Sechita and for
> the rest of the poem dances out
> Sechita's life.

sechita had heard these things/ she moved
as if she'd known them/ the silver n high-toned laughin/
the violins n marble floors/ sechita pushed the clingin
delta dust wit painted toes/ the patch-work tent waz
poka-dotted/ stale lights snatched at the shadows/ creole

carnival waz playin natchez in ten minutes/ her splendid
red garters/ gin-stained n itchy on her thigh/ blk-diamond
stockings darned wit yellow threads/ an ol starched taffeta
can-can fell abundantly orange/ from her waist round the
splinterin chair/ sechita/ egyptian/ goddess of creativity/
2nd millennium/ threw her heavy hair in a coil over her neck/
sechita/ goddess/ the recordin of history/ spread crimson oil
on her cheeks/ waxed her eyebrows/ n unconsciously slugged
the last hard whiskey in the glass/ the broken mirror she
used to decorate her face/ made her forehead tilt backwards/
her cheeks appear sunken/ her sassy chin only large enuf/
to keep her full lower lip/ from growin into her neck/ sechita/
had learned to make allowances for the distortions/
but the heavy dust of the delta/ left a tinge of grit n
darkness/ on every one of her dresses/ on her arms & her
shoulders/ sechita/ waz anxious to get back to st. louis/
the dirt there didnt crawl from the earth into yr soul/
at least/ in st. louis/ the grime waz store bought
second-hand/ here in natchez/ god seemed to be wipin his
feet in her face/

one of the wrestlers had finally won
tonite/ the mulatto/ raul/ was sposed to hold the boomin
half-caste/ searin eagle/ in a bear hug/ 8 counts/ get
thrown unawares/ fall out the ring/ n then do searin eagle
in for good/ sechita/ cd hear redneck whoops n slappin on
the back/ she gathered her sparsely sequined skirts/ tugged
the waist cincher from under her greyin slips/ n made her face

immobile/ she made her face like nefertiti/ approachin her
own tomb/ she suddenly threw/ her leg full-force/ thru the
canvas curtain/ a deceptive glass stone/ sparkled/ malignant
on her ankle/ her calf waz tauntin in the brazen carnie
lights/ the full moon/ sechita/ goddess/ of love/ egypt/
2nd millennium/ performin the rites/ the conjurin of men/
conjurin the spirit/ in natchez/ the mississippi spewed
a heavy fume of barely movin waters/ sechita's legs slashed
furiously thru the cracker nite/ & gold pieces hittin the
makeshift stage/ her thighs/ they were aimin coins tween her
thighs/ sechita/ egypt/ goddess/ harmony/ kicked viciously
thru the nite/ catchin stars tween her toes.

> *The lady in green exits into the stage left volm, the lady in purple exits into up stage left.*
>
> *The lady in brown enters from up stage right.*

    lady in brown
de library waz right down from de trolly tracks
cross from de laundry-mat
thru de big shinin floors & granite pillars
ol st. louis is famous for
i found toussaint
but not til after months uv
cajun katie/ pippi longstockin

christopher robin/ eddie heyward & a pooh bear
in the children's room
only pioneer girls & magic rabbits
& big city white boys
i knew i waznt sposedta
but i ran inta the ADULT READING ROOM
        & came across

        TOUSSAINT

        my first blk man
(i never counted george washington carver
cuz i didnt like peanuts)
        still
TOUSSAINT waz a blk man a negro like my mama say
who refused to be a slave
& he spoke french
& didnt low no white man to tell him nothin
    not napolean
    not maximillien
    not robespierre

TOUSSAINT L'OUVERTURE
waz the beginnin uv reality for me
in the summer contest for
who colored child can read
15 books in three weeks
i won & raved abt TOUSSAINT L'OUVERTURE
at the afternoon ceremony

  waz disqualified
    cuz Toussaint
      belonged in the ADULT READING ROOM
     & i cried
& carried dead Toussaint home in the book
he waz dead & livin to me
cuz TOUSSAINT & them
they held the citadel gainst the french
wid the spirits of ol dead africans from outta the ground
TOUSSAINT led they army of zombies
walkin cannon ball shootin spirits to free Haiti
& they waznt slaves no more

      TOUSSAINT L'OUVERTURE
became my secret lover at the age of 8
i entertained him in my bedroom
widda flashlight under my covers
way inta the night/ we discussed strategies
how to remove white girls from my hopscotch games
& etc.
TOUSSAINT
waz layin in bed wit me next to raggedy ann
the night i decided to run away from my
    integrated home
     integrated street
      integrated school
1955 waz not a good year for lil blk girls

Toussaint said 'lets go to haiti'

i said 'awright'
& packed some very important things in a brown paper bag
so i wdnt haveta come back
then Toussaint & i took the hodiamont streetcar
to the river
last stop
only 15¢
cuz there waznt nobody cd see Toussaint cept me
& we walked all down thru north st. louis
where the french settlers usedta live
in tiny brick houses all huddled together
wit barely missin windows & shingles uneven
wit colored kids playin & women on low porches sippin beer

i cd talk to Toussaint down by the river
like this waz where we waz gonna stow away
on a boat for new orleans
& catch a creole fishin-rig for port-au-prince
then we waz just gonna read & talk all the time
& eat fried bananas
                        we waz just walkin & skippin past ol drunk men
when dis ol young boy jumped out at me sayin
'HEY GIRL YA BETTAH COME OVAH HEAH N TALK TO ME'
well
i turned to TOUSSAINT (who waz furious)
& i shouted
'ya silly ol boy
ya bettah leave me alone

or TOUSSAINT'S gonna get yr ass'
de silly ol boy came round de corner laughin all in my face
'yellah gal
ya sure must be somebody to know my name so quick'
i waz disgusted
& wanted to get on to haiti
widout some tacky ol boy botherin me
still he kept standin there
kickin milk cartons & bits of brick
tryin to get all in my business
                i mumbled to L'OUVERTURE 'what shd I do'
finally
i asked this silly ol boy
'WELL WHO ARE YOU?'
he say
'MY NAME IS TOUSSAINT JONES'
well
i looked right at him
those skidded out cordoroy pants
a striped teashirt wid holes in both elbows
a new scab over his left eye
& i said
                'what's yr name again'
he say
'i'm toussaint jones'
'wow
i am on my way to see
TOUSSAINT L'OUVERTURE in HAITI

are ya any kin to him
he dont take no stuff from no white folks
& they gotta country all they own
& there aint no slaves'
that silly ol boy squinted his face all up
'looka heah girl
i am TOUSSAINT JONES
& i'm right heah lookin at ya
& i dont take no stuff from no white folks
ya dont see none round heah do ya?'
& he sorta pushed out his chest
then he say
'come on   lets go on down to the docks
& look at the boats'
i waz real puzzled goin down to the docks
wit my paper bag & my books
i felt TOUSSAINT L'OUVERTURE sorta leave me
& i waz sad
til i realized
TOUSSAINT JONES waznt too different
from TOUSSAINT L'OUVERTURE
cept the ol one waz in haiti
& this one wid me speakin english & eatin apples
yeah.
toussaint jones waz awright wit me
no tellin what all spirits we cd move
down by the river
st. louis 1955   hey wait.

30/

> *The lady in brown exits into the stage right volm.*
>
> *The lady in red enters from the stage left volm.*

    lady in red
orange butterflies & aqua sequins
ensconsed tween slight bosoms
silk roses dartin from behind her ears
the passion flower of southwest los angeles
meandered down hoover street
past dark shuttered houses where
women from louisiana shelled peas
round 3:00 & sent their sons
whistlin to the store for fatback & black-eyed peas
she glittered in heat
& seemed to be lookin for rides
when she waznt & absolutely
eyed every man who waznt lame white or noddin out
she let her thigh slip from her skirt
crossin the street
she slowed to be examined
& she never looked back to smile
or acknowledge a sincere 'hey mama'
or to meet the eyes of someone
purposely findin sometin to do in

      her direction
            she waz sullen
            & the rhinestones etchin the corners of her mouth
            suggested tears
            fresh kisses that had done no good
she always wore her stomach out
lined with small iridescent feathers
the hairs round her navel seemed to dance
& she didnt let on
she knew
from behind her waist waz aching to be held
the pastel ivy drawn on her shoulders
to be brushed with lips & fingers
smellin of honey & jack daniels
            she waz hot
            a deliberate coquette
            who never did without
            what she wanted
& she wanted to be unforgettable
she wanted to be a memory
a wound   to every man
arragant enough to want her
            she waz the wrath
              of women in windows
                  fingerin shades/ ol lace curtains
                camoflagin despair &
              stretch marks
so she glittered honestly

delighted she waz desired
& allowed those especially
schemin/ tactful suitors
to experience her body & spirit
tearin/ so easily blendin with theirs/
& they were so happy
& lay on her lime sheets full & wet
from her tongue   she kissed
them reverently   even ankles
edges of beards . . .

> *The stage goes to darkness except*
> *for a special on the lady in red,*
> *who lies motionless on the floor; as*
> *the lights slowly fade up the lady*
> *in red sits up.*

at 4:30 AM
she rose
movin the arms & legs that trapped her
she sighed affirmin the sculptured man
& made herself a bath
of dark musk oil egyptian crystals
& florida water to remove his smell
to wash away the glitter
to watch the butterflies melt into
suds & the rhinestones fall beneath
her buttocks like smooth pebbles

in a missouri creek
layin in water
she became herself
ordinary
brown braided woman
with big legs & full lips
reglar
seriously intendin to finish her
night's work
she quickly walked to her guest
straddled on her pillows & began
        'you'll have to go now/ i've
        a lot of work to do/ & i cant
        with a man around/ here are yr pants/
        there's coffee on the stove/ its been
        very nice/ but i cant see you again/
        you got what you came for/ didnt you'
& she smiled
he wd either mumble curses bout crazy bitches
or sit dumbfounded
while she repeated
        'i cdnt possibly wake up/ with
        a strange man in my bed/ why
        dont you go home'
she cda been slapped upside the head
or verbally challenged
but she never waz
& the ones who fell prey to the

dazzle of hips painted with
orange blossoms & magnolia scented wrists
had wanted no more
than to lay between her sparklin thighs
& had planned on leavin before dawn
& she had been so divine
devastatingly bizarre the way
her mouth fit round
& now she stood a
reglar colored girl
fulla the same malice
livid indifference as a sistah
worn from supportin a wd be hornplayer
or waitin by the window
              & they knew
              & left in a hurry
she wd gather her tinsel &
jewels from the tub
& laugh gayly or vengeful
she stored her silk roses by her bed
& when she finished writin
the account of her exploit in a diary
embroidered with lilies & moonstones
she placed the rose behind her ear
& cried herself to sleep.

All the lights fade except for a special on the lady in red; the lady in red exits into the stage left volm.

The lady in blue enters from up right.

    lady in blue
i usedta live in the world
then i moved to HARLEM
& my universe is now six blocks

when i walked in the pacific
i imagined waters ancient from accra/ tunis
cleansin me/ feedin me
now my ankles are coated in grey filth
from the puddle neath the hydrant

my oceans were life
what waters i have here sit stagnant
circlin ol men's bodies
shit & broken lil whiskey bottles
left to make me bleed

i usedta live in the world
now i live in harlem & my universe is six blocks
a tunnel with a train
i can ride anywhere
remaining a stranger

NO MAN YA CANT GO WIT ME/ I DONT EVEN
KNOW YOU/ NO/ I DONT WANNA KISS YOU/
YOU AINT BUT 12 YRS OLD/ NO MAN/ PLEASE
PLEASE PLEASE LEAVE ME ALONE/ TOMORROW/ YEAH/
NO/ PLEASE/ I CANT USE IT
   i cd stay alone
   a woman in the world
   then i moved to
HARLEM
i come in at dusk
stay close to the curb

                       The lady in yellow enters, she's
                       waiting for a bus.

round midnite
praying wont no young man
think i'm pretty in a dark mornin

                       The lady in purple enters, she's
                       waiting for a bus.

wdnt be good
not good at all
to meet a tall short black brown young man fulla his power
in the dark
in my universe of six blocks
straight up brick walls
women hangin outta windows

like ol silk stockings
cats cryin/ children gigglin/ a tavern wit red curtains
bad smells/ kissin ladies smilin & dirt
sidewalks spittin/ men cursing/ playin

> *The lady in orange enters, she is
> being followed by a man, the
> lady in blue becomes that man.*

'I SPENT MORE MONEY YESTERDAY
THAN THE DAY BEFORE & ALL THAT'S MORE N YOU
NIGGAH EVER GOTTA HOLD TO
COME OVER HERE BITCH
CANT YA SEE THIS IS $5'

never mind sister
dont pay him no mind
go go go go go go sister
do yr thing
never mind

i usedta live in the world
really be in the world
free & sweet talkin
good mornin & thank-you & nice day
uh huh
i cant now
i cant be nice to nobody

nice is such a rip-off
reglar beauty & a smile in the street
is just a set-up

i usedta be in the world
a woman in the world
i hadda right to the world
then i moved to harlem
for the set-up
a universe
six blocks of cruelty
piled up on itself
a tunnel
closin

> *The four ladies on stage freeze, count 4, then the ladies in blue, purple, yellow and orange move to their places for the next poem.*

    lady in purple
three of us like a pyramid
three friends
one laugh
one music
one flowered shawl
knotted on each neck

we all saw him at the same time
& he saw us
i felt a quick thump in each one of us
didnt know what to do
we all wanted what waz comin our way
so we split
but he found one
& she loved him

the other two were tickled
& spurned his advances
when the one who loved him waz somewhere else
he wd come to her saying
yr friends love you very much
i have tried
& they keep askin where are you
she smiled
wonderin how long her friends
wd hold out
he waz what they were lookin for
he bided his time
he waited til romance waned
the three of us made up stories
bout usedta & cda been nice
the season waz dry
no men
no quickies
not one dance or eyes unrelentin

one day after another
cept for the one who loved him
he appeared irregularly
expectin graciousness no matter what
she cut fresh strawberries
her friends callt less frequently
went on hunts for passin fancies
she cdnt figure out what waz happenin
then the rose
she left by his pillow
she found on her friends desk
& there waz nothing to say
she said
i wanna tell you
he's been after me
all the time
says he's free & can explain
what's happenin wit you
is nothin to me
& i dont wanna hurt you
but you know i need someone now
& you know
how wonderful he is

her friend cdnt speak or cry
they hugged & went to where he waz
wit another woman
he said good-bye to one

tol the other he wd call
he smiled a lot

she held her head on her lap
the lap of her sisters soakin up tears
each understandin how much love stood between them
how much love between them
love between them
love like sisters

> *Sharp music is heard, each lady
> dances as if catching a disease from
> the lady next to her, suddenly
> they all freeze.*

lady in orange
ever since i realized there waz someone callt
a colored girl an evil woman a bitch or a nag
i been tryin not to be that & leave bitterness
in somebody else's cup/ come to somebody to love me
without deep & nasty smellin scald from lye or bein
left screamin in a street fulla lunatics/ whisperin
slut bitch bitch niggah/ get outta here wit alla that/
i didnt have any of that for you/ i brought you what joy
i found & i found joy/ honest fingers round my face/ with
dead musicians on 78's from cuba/ or live musicians on five
dollar lp's from chicago/ where i have never been/ & i love
willie colon & arsenio rodriquez/ especially cuz i can make

the music loud enuf/ so there is no me but dance/ & when
i can dance like that/ there's nothin cd hurt me/ but
i get tired & i haveta come offa the floor & then there's
that woman who hurt you/ who you left/ three or four times/
& just went back/ after you put my heart in the bottom of
yr shoe/ you just walked back to where you hurt/ & i didnt
have nothin/ so i went to where somebody had somethin for me/
but he waznt you/ & i waz on the way back from her house
in the bottom of yr shoe/ so this is not a love poem/ cuz there
are only memorial albums available/ & even charlie mingus
wanted desperately to be a pimp/ & i wont be able to see eddie
palmieri for months/ so this is a requium for myself/ cuz i
have died in a real way/ not wid aqua coffins & du-wop cadillacs/
i used to joke abt when i waz messin round/ but a real dead
lovin is here for you now/ cuz i dont know anymore/ how
to avoid my own face wet wit my tears/ cuz i had convinced
myself colored girls had no right to sorrow/ & i lived
& loved that way & kept sorrow on the curb/ allegedly
for you/ but i know i did it for myself/
i cdnt stand it
i cdnt stand bein sorry & colored at the same time
it's so redundant in the modern world

   lady in purple
i lived wit myths & music waz my ol man & i cd dance
a dance outta time/ a dance wit no partners/ take my
pills & keep right on steppin/ linger in non-english
speakin arms so there waz no possibility of understandin

& you YOU
came sayin i am the niggah/ i am the baddest muthafuckah
out there/
i said yes/ this is who i am waitin for
& to come wit you/ i hadta bring everythin
the dance & the terror
the dead musicians & the hope
& those scars i had hidden wit smiles & good fuckin
lay open
& i dont know i dont know any more tricks
i am really colored & really sad sometimes & you hurt me
more than i ever danced outta/ into oblivion isnt far enuf
to get outta this/ i am ready to die like a lily in the
desert/ & i cdnt let you in on it cuz i didnt know/ here
is what i have/ poems/ big thighs/ lil tits/ &
so much love/ will you take it from me this one time/
please this is for you/ arsenio's tres cleared the way
& makes me pure again/ please please/ this is for you
i want you to love me/ let me love you/ i dont wanna
dance wit ghosts/ snuggle lovers i made up in my drunkenness/
lemme love you just like i am/ a colored girl/ i'm finally bein
real/ no longer symmetrical & impervious to pain

   lady in blue   *change?*
we deal wit emotion too much
so why dont we go on ahead & be white then/
& make everythin dry & abstract wit no rhythm & no
reelin for sheer sensual pleasure/ yes let's go on

& be white/ we're right in the middle of it/ no use
holdin out/ holdin onto ourselves/ lets think our
way outta feelin/ lets abstract ourselves some families
& maybe maybe tonite/ i'll find a way to make myself
come witout you/ no fingers or other objects just thot
which isnt spiritual evolution cuz its empty & godliness
is plenty is ripe & fertile/ thinkin wont do me a bit of
good tonite/ i need to be loved/ & havent the audacity
to say
where are you/ & dont know who to say it to

lady in yellow
i've lost it
touch wit reality/ i dont know who's doin it
i thot i waz but i waz so stupid i waz able to be hurt
& that's not real/ not anymore/ i shd be immune/ if i'm
still alive & that's what i waz discussin/ how i am still
alive & my dependency on other livin beins for love
i survive on intimacy & tomorrow/ that's all i've got goin
& the music waz like smack & you knew abt that
& still refused my dance waz not enuf/ & it waz all i had
but bein alive & bein a woman & bein colored is a metaphysical
dilemma/ i havent conquered yet/ do you see the point
my spirit is too ancient to understand the separation of
soul & gender/ my love is too delicate to have thrown
back on my face

*The ladies in red, green, and brown
enter quietly; in the background
all of the ladies except the lady in
yellow are frozen; the lady in
yellow looks at them, walks by
them, touches them; they do not
move.*

    lady in yellow
my love is too delicate to have thrown back on my face

*The lady in yellow starts to exit
into the stage right volm. Just as she
gets to the volm, the lady in brown
comes to life.*

    lady in brown
my love is too beautiful to have thrown back on my face

    lady in purple
my love is too sanctified to have thrown back on my face

    lady in blue
my love is too magic to have thrown back on my face

    lady in orange
my love is too saturday nite to have thrown back on my face

    lady in red
my love is too complicated to have thrown back on my face

    lady in green
my love is too music to have thrown back on my face

    everyone
music
music

> *The lady in green then breaks into a dance, the other ladies follow her lead and soon they are all dancing and chanting together.*

    lady in green
yank dankka dank dank

    everyone
music

    lady in green
yank dankka dank dank

    everyone
music

    lady in green
yank dankka dank dank

  everyone (but started by the lady in yellow)
delicate
delicate
delicate

  everyone (but started by the lady in brown)
and beautiful
and beautiful
and beautiful

  everyone (but started by the lady in purple)
oh sanctified
oh sanctified
oh sanctified

  everyone (but started by the lady in blue)
magic
magic
magic

  everyone (but started by the lady in orange)
and saturday nite
and saturday nite
and saturday nite

  everyone (but started by the lady in red)
and complicated
and complicated

   and complicated
   and complicated
   and complicated
   and complicated
   and complicated
   and complicated

The dance reaches a climax and all of the ladies fall out tired, but full of life and togetherness.

    lady in green
somebody almost walked off wid alla my stuff
not my poems or a dance i gave up in the street
but somebody almost walked off wid alla my stuff
like a kleptomaniac workin hard & forgettin while stealin
this is mine/ this aint yr stuff/
now why dont you put me back & let me hang out in my own self
somebody almost walked off wid alla my stuff
& didnt care enuf to send a note home sayin
i waz late for my solo conversation
or two sizes too small for my own tacky skirts
what can anybody do wit somethin of no value on
a open market/ did you getta dime for my things/
hey man/ where are you goin wid alla my stuff/
this is a woman's trip & i need my stuff/
to ohh & ahh abt/ daddy/ i gotta mainline number
from my own shit/ now wontchu put me back/ & let

me play this duet/ wit this silver ring in my nose/
honest to god/ somebody almost run off wit alla my stuff/
& i didnt bring anythin but the kick & sway of it
the perfect ass for my man & none of it is theirs
this is mine/ ntozake 'her own things'/ that's my name/
now give me my stuff/ i see ya hidin my laugh/ & how i
sit wif my legs open sometimes/ to give my crotch
some sunlight/ & there goes my love my toes my chewed
up finger nails/ niggah/ wif the curls in yr hair/
mr. louisiana hot link/ i want my stuff back/
my rhythms & my voice/ open my mouth/ & let me talk ya
outta/ throwin my shit in the sewar/ this is some delicate
leg & whimsical kiss/ i gotta have to give to my choice/
without you runnin off wit alla my shit/
now you cant have me less i give me away/ & i waz
doin all that/ til ya run off on a good thing/
who is this you left me wit/ some simple bitch
widda bad attitude/ i wants my things/
i want my arm wit the hot iron scar/ & my leg wit the
flea bite/ i want my calloused feet & quik language back
in my mouth/ fried plantains/ pineapple pear juice/
sun-ra & joseph & jules/ i want my own things/ how i lived them/
& give me my memories/ how i waz when i waz there/
you cant have them or do nothin wit them/
stealin my shit from me/ dont make it yrs/ makes it stolen/
somebody almost run off wit alla my stuff/ & i waz standin
there/ lookin at myself/ the whole time
& it waznt a spirit took my stuff/ waz a man whose

ego walked round like Rodan's shadow/ waz a man faster
n my innocence/ waz a lover/ i made too much
room for/ almost run off wit alla my stuff/
& i didnt know i'd give it up so quik/ & the one running wit it/
dont know he got it/ & i'm shoutin this is mine/ & he dont
know he got it/ my stuff is the anonymous ripped off treasure
of the year/ did you know somebody almost got away with me/
me in a plastic bag under their arm/ me
danglin on a string of personal carelessness/ i'm spattered wit
mud & city rain/ & no i didnt get a chance to take a douche/
hey man/ this is not your perogative/ i gotta have me in my
pocket/ to get round like a good woman shd/ & make the poem
in the pot or the chicken in the dance/ what i got to do/
i gotta have my stuff to do it to/
why dont ya find yr own things/ & leave this package
of me for my destiny/ what ya got to get from me/
i'll give it to ya/ yeh/ i'll give it to ya/
round 5:00 in the winter/ when the sky is blue-red/
& Dew City is gettin pressed/ if it's really my stuff/
ya gotta give it to me/ if ya really want it/ i'm
the only one/ can handle it

   lady in blue
that niggah will be back tomorrow, sayin 'i'm sorry'

   lady in yellow
get this, last week my ol man came in sayin, 'i don't know
how she got yr number baby, i'm sorry'

> *lady in brown*

no this one is it, 'o baby, ya know i waz high, i'm sorry'

> *lady in purple*

'i'm only human, and inadequacy is what makes us human, &
if we was perfect we wdnt have nothin to strive for, so you
might as well go on and forgive me pretty baby, cause i'm sorry'

> *lady in green*

'shut up bitch, i told you i waz sorry'

> *lady in orange*

no this one is it, 'i do ya like i do ya cause i thot
ya could take it, now i'm sorry'

> *lady in red*

'now i know that ya know i love ya, but i aint ever gonna
love ya like ya want me to love ya, i'm sorry'

> *lady in blue*

one thing i dont need
is any more apologies
i got sorry greetin me at my front door
you can keep yrs
i dont know what to do wit em
they dont open doors
or bring the sun back
they dont make me happy

or get a mornin paper
didnt nobody stop usin my tears to wash cars
cuz a sorry

i am simply tired
of collectin
        i didnt know
        i was so important toyou'
i'm gonna haveta throw some away
i cant get to the clothes in my closet
for alla the sorries
i'm gonna tack a sign to my door
leave a message by the phone
        'if you called
        to say yr sorry
        call somebody
        else
        i dont use em anymore'
i let sorry/ didnt meanta/ & how cd i know abt that
take a walk down a dark & musty street in brooklyn
i'm gonna do exactly what i want to
& i wont be sorry for none of it
letta sorry soothe yr soul/ i'm gonna soothe mine

you were always inconsistent
doin somethin & then bein sorry
beatin my heart to death
talkin bout you sorry

well
i will not call
i'm not goin to be nice
i will raise my voice
& scream & holler
& break things & race the engine
& tell all yr secrets bout yrself to yr face
& i will list in detail everyone of my wonderful lovers
& their ways
i will play oliver lake
loud
& i wont be sorry for none of it

i loved you on purpose
i was open on purpose
i still crave vulnerability & close talk
& i'm not even sorry bout you bein sorry
you can carry all the guilt & grime ya wanna
just dont give it to me
i cant use another sorry
next time
you should admit
you're mean/ low-down/ triflin/ & no count straight out
steada bein sorry alla the time
enjoy bein yrself

lady in red
there waz no air/ the sheets made ripples under his
body like crumpled paper napkins in a summer park/ & lil
specks of somethin from tween his toes or the biscuits
from the day before ran in the sweat that tucked the sheet
into his limbs like he waz an ol frozen bundle of chicken/
& he'd get up to make coffee, drink wine, drink water/ he
wished one of his friends who knew where he waz wd come by
with some blow or some shit/ anythin/ there waz no air/
he'd see the spotlights in the alleyways downstairs movin
in the air/ cross his wall over his face/ & get under the
covers & wait for an all clear or til he cd hear traffic
again/

there waznt nothin wrong with him/ there waznt nothin wrong
with him/ he kept tellin crystal/
any niggah wanna kill vietnamese children more n stay home
& raise his own is sicker than a rabid dog/
that's how their thing had been goin since he got back/
crystal just got inta sayin whatta fool niggah beau waz
& always had been/ didnt he go all over uptown sayin the
child waznt his/ waz some no counts bastard/ & any ol city
police cd come & get him if they wanted/ cuz as soon as
the blood type & shit waz together/ everybody wd know that
crystal waz a no good lyin whore/ and this after she'd been
his girl since she waz thirteen/ when he caught her
on the stairway/

he came home crazy as hell/ he tried to get veterans benefits

to go to school & they kept right on puttin him in
remedial classes/ he cdnt read wortha damn/ so beau
cused the teachers of holdin him back & got himself
a gypsy cab to drive/ but his cab kept breakin
down/ & the cops was always messin wit him/ plus not
gettin much bread/

& crystal went & got pregnant again/ beau most beat
her to death when she tol him/ she still gotta scar
under her right tit where he cut her up/ still crystal
went right on & had the baby/ so now beau willie had
two children/ a little girl/ naomi kenya & a boy/ kwame beau
willie brown/ & there waz no air/

how in the hell did he get in this mess anyway/ somebody
went & tol crystal that beau waz spendin alla his money
on the bartendin bitch down at the merry-go-round cafe/
beau sat straight up in the bed/ wrapped up in the sheets
lookin like john the baptist or a huge baby wit stubble
& nuts/ now he hadta get alla that shit outta crystal's
mind/ so she wd let him come home/ crystal had gone &
got a court order saying beau willie brown had no access
to his children/ if he showed his face he waz subject
to arrest/ shit/ she'd been in his ass to marry her
since she waz 14 years old & here when she 22/ she wanna
throw him out cuz he say he'll marry her/ she burst
out laughin/ hollerin whatchu wanna marry me for now/
so i can support yr

ass/ or come sit wit ya when they lock yr behind
up/ cause they gonna come for ya/ ya goddamn lunatic/
they gonna come/ & i'm not gonna have a thing to do
wit it/ o no i wdnt marry yr pitiful black ass for
nothin & she went on to bed/

the next day beau willie came in blasted & got ta swingin
chairs at crystal/ who cdnt figure out what the hell
he waz doin/ til he got ta shoutin bout how she waz gonna
marry him/ & get some more veterans benefits/ & he cd
stop drivin them crazy spics round/ while they tryin
to kill him for $15/ beau waz sweatin terrible/ beatin
on crystal/ & he cdnt do no more with the table n chairs/
so he went to get the high chair/ & lil kwame waz in it/
& beau waz beatin crystal with the high chair & her son/
& some notion got inta him to stop/ and he run out/

crystal most died/ that's why the police wdnt low
beau near where she lived/ & she'd been tellin the kids
their daddy tried to kill her & kwame/ & he just wanted
to marry her/ that's what/ he wanted to marry her/ &
have a family/ but the bitch waz crazy/ beau willie
waz sittin in this hotel in his drawers drinkin
coffee & wine in the heat of the day spillin shit all
over hisself/ laughin/ bout how he waz gonna get crystal
to take him back/ & let him be a man in the house/ & she
wdnt even have to go to work no more/ he got dressed
all up in his ivory shirt & checkered pants to go see

crystal & get this mess all cleared up/
he knocked on the door to crystal's rooms/ & she
didnt answer/ he beat on the door & crystal & naomi
started cryin/ beau gotta shoutin again how he wanted
to marry her/ & waz she always gonna be a whore/ or
did she wanna husband/ & crystal just kept on
screamin for him to leave us alone/ just leave us
alone/ so beau broke the door down/ crystal held
the children in fronta her/ she picked kwame off the
floor/ in her arms/ & she held naomi by her shoulders/
& kept on sayin/ beau willie brown/ get outta here/
the police is gonna come for ya/ ya fool/ get outta here/
do you want the children to see you act the fool again/
you want kwame to brain damage from you throwin him
round/ niggah/ get outta here/ get out & dont show yr
ass again or i'll kill ya/ i swear i'll kill ya/
he reached for naomi/ crystal grabbed the lil girl &
stared at beau willie like he waz a leper or somethin/
dont you touch my children/ muthafucker/ or i'll kill
you/

beau willie jumped back all humble & apologetic/ i'm
sorry/ i dont wanna hurt em/ i just wanna hold em &
get on my way/ i dont wanna cuz you no more trouble/
i wanted to marry you & give ya things
what you gonna give/ a broken jaw/ niggah get outta here/
he ignored crystal's outburst & sat down motionin for
naomi to come to him/ she smiled back at her daddy/

crystal felt naomi givin in & held her tighter/
naomi/ pushed away & ran to her daddy/ cryin/ daddy, daddy
come back daddy/ come back/ but be nice to mommy/
cause mommy loves you/ and ya gotta be nice/
he sat her on his knee/ & played with her ribbons &
they counted fingers & toes/ every so often he
looked over to crystal holdin kwame/ like a statue/
& he'd say/ see crystal/ i can be a good father/
now let me see my son/ & she didnt move/ &
he coaxed her & he coaxed her/ tol her she waz
still a hot lil ol thing & pretty & strong/ didnt
she get right up after that lil ol fight they had
& go back to work/ beau willie oozed kindness &
crystal who had known so lil/ let beau hold kwame/

as soon as crystal let the baby outta her arms/ beau
jumped up a laughin & a gigglin/ a hootin & a hollerin/
awright bitch/ awright bitch/ you gonna marry me/
you gonna marry me . . .
i aint gonna marry ya/ i aint ever gonna marry ya/
for nothin/ you gonna be in the jail/ you gonna be
under the jail for this/ now gimme my kids/ ya give
me back my kids/

he kicked the screen outta the window/ & held the kids
offa the sill/ you gonna marry me/ yeh, i'll marry ya/
anything/ but bring the children back in the house/
he looked from where the kids were hangin from the

fifth story/ at alla the people screamin at him/ &
he started sweatin again/ say to alla the neighbors/
you gonna marry me/

i stood by beau in the window/ with naomi reachin
for me/ & kwame screamin mommy mommy from the fifth
story/ but i cd only whisper/ & he dropped em

    lady in red
i waz missin somethin

    lady in purple
somethin so important

    lady in orange
somethin promised

    lady in blue
a layin on of hands

    lady in green
fingers near my forehead

    lady in yellow
strong

    lady in green
cool

    lady in orange
movin

    lady in purple
makin me whole

    lady in orange
sense

    lady in green
pure

    lady in blue
all the gods comin into me
layin me open to myself

    lady in red
i waz missin somethin

    lady in green
somethin promised

lady in orange
somethin free

lady in purple
a layin on of hands

lady in blue
i know bout/ layin on bodies/ layin outta man
bringin him alla my fleshy self & some of my pleasure
bein taken full eager wet like i get sometimes
i waz missin somethin

lady in purple
a layin on of hands

lady in blue
not a man

lady in yellow
layin on

lady in purple
not my mama/ holdin me tight/ sayin
i'm always gonna be her girl
not a layin on of bosom & womb
a layin on of hands
the holiness of myself released

    lady in *red*
i sat up one nite walkin a boardin house
screamin/ cryin/ the ghost of another woman
who waz missin what i waz missin
i wanted to jump up outta my bones
& be done wit myself
leave me alone
& go on in the wind
it waz too much
i fell into a numbness
til the only tree i cd see
took me up in her branches
held me in the breeze
made me dawn dew
that chill at daybreak
the sun wrapped me up swingin rose light everywhere
the sky laid over me like a million men
i waz cold/ i waz burnin up/ a child
& endlessly weavin garments for the moon
wit my tears

i found god in myself
& i loved her/ i loved her fiercely

                              All of the ladies repeat to them-
                              selves softly the lines 'i found god
                              in myself & i loved her.' It soon
                              becomes a song of joy, started by

the lady in blue. The ladies sing first to each other, then gradually to the audience. After the song peaks the ladies enter into a closed tight circle.

    lady in brown
& this is for colored girls who have considered
suicide/ but are movin to the ends of their own
rainbows